T0113593

Mohammed Umar was born in Azare in Nigeria's Bauchi State. He studied journalism in Moscow (1991) and political economy in London (1995). Mohammed Umar served as a judge for the Caine Prize for African Writing in 2009 and he was the winner of the Muslim News Award for Excellence in Arts in 2010. His books have been translated into over sixty languages. He lives in London.

ALSO BY MOHAMMED UMAR

SUNSET AT DAWN

A Play about Refugees
in Three Acts

by
Mohammed Umar

First published in Great Britain 2019
Salaam Publishing
London

www.salaampublishing.com
salaampublishing@gmail.com

ISBN 978-1-912450-17-6 (Paperback)

LIST OF CHARACTERS

FIRST MINISTER

DEFENCE MINISTER

SECRETARY OF STATE

ONE POLICEMAN

FIVE FAJRIS INCLUDING AN OLD MAN

FIVE FOREIGNERS

ACT ONE
SCENE I

The stage is divided into three parts. The top part is smaller, brightly lit and empty. There is a sign: **CITY IN THE SKY**. *The middle part of the stage is wider, well-lit and has a sign:* **FAJRA – THE BLESSED PLATEAU**. *The lower part is below the stage, at the same level as the front row seat. It is narrow, small and dark. There is a sign:* **THE VALLEY**.

Action takes place in **FAJRA**.

Time: **THE PRESENT**

There is a table, two chairs, a computer, a flag and a sign: **OFFICE OF THE FIRST MINISTER**.

The curtain rises, revealing **ONE POLICEMAN** *standing guard at the door leading to the stage. A well-dressed man, holding a mobile phone walks in. The* **POLICEMAN** *salutes. He does not respond. He crosses the stage, looking at his mobile phone till he gets to the desk and sits down.*

VOICE: (*backstage*) Is the First Minister in?

POLICEMAN: (*saluting the man entering stage*) Yes sir.

FIRST MINISTER: (*stands up upon seeing the man, smiles*) Ah! Defence Minister. How nice to see you.

DEFENCE MINISTER: Have you seen my urgent message?

FIRST MINISTER: Yes I have seen it. (*showing him his mobile phone*) What is more, I have seen them with my own eyes. (*pointing to the valley*)

DEFENCE MINISTER: So what's your decision?

FIRST MINISTER: Well, nothing definitive yet.

DEFENCE MINISTER: You asked for some time to think about it.

FIRST MINISTER: Yes I did but …

DEFENCE MINISTER: (*interrupts*) Sorry, but their presence there is making Fajris very anxious.

FIRST MINISTER: I understand but there is no need for anyone to be anxious. You should reassure them that a meaningful decision will be taken...

DEFENCE MINISTER: (*interrupts*) There are a lot of Fajris who are really worried out there.

FIRST MINISTER: (*with calm authority*) As a member of the Supreme Council and a Custodian of Fajra I am aware of my responsibilities.

DEFENCE MINISTER: (*turns to audience*) As you must have guessed, we have a problem here in Fajra. Yesterday two foreigners were spotted in the valley. (*points to the valley*) This has got the people of Fajra talking. According to those who saw them, the foreigners are so strange looking it scared the hell out of people. Those who spoke to them said that, apart from their shape, the way they spoke and thought was so distant from ours as to be inhuman. I'm still receiving messages from people who've been unable to sleep because of them. (*walks to the edge of the plateau, looks down*)

> *Light shines on the valley.* **TWO MEN** *and a* **WOMAN,** *all very short and all wearing blue clothes are seen standing, looking at the plateau. They hold a sign:* **REFUGEES SEEKING ASYLUM**

DEFENCE MINISTER: (*continues*) Look! Yesterday there were only two, today there are three of them. Can you imagine how many there'll be in a year's time if the numbers keep increasing at this rate?

FIRST MINISTER: I've told you there's no need to panic.

DEFENCE MINISTER: I'm not panicking, I'm simply stating the obvious. We don't know if there are more foreigners coming but we can assume it's likely, and if so, we have a duty to protect our beloved town and people from this threat.

FIRST MINISTER: What do you mean by threat?

DEFENCE MINISTER: They're a threat because more will come...

FIRST MINISTER: While I agree with you that that might create a problem, I think we can manage whatever problem arises from their coming...I need more time ...

DEFENCE MINISTER: (*turns sharply, interrupts*) Why have you changed your mind? At the meeting of the Custodians yesterday you were eager to get rid of them first thing in the morning. Now you're talking about giving you more time and managing the problem. What happened to you overnight?

    FIRST MINISTER *does not answer.*

DEFENCE MINISTER: (*continues*) We cannot be changing our minds on such serious issues when the facts on the ground demand quick and decisive action.

FIRST MINISTER: (*calmly*) I simply want to make sure I make the right decision.

DEFENCE MINISTER: Fajra is about to be invaded and you...

FIRST MINISTER: (*holds the hand of* **DEFENCE MINISTER** *and leads him to the edge of the plateau*) Three small people don't look like an invasion to me.

DEFENCE MINISTER: They may be small but we don't know if they're armed or if they intend to do us harm. We should err on the side of caution. Just because they hold a sign saying they are refugees doesn't mean we should believe them. It could be a disguise. (*Pause*) We certainly don't want them squatting on our land in the valley.

FIRST MINISTER: Why are you worried about that?

DEFENCE MINISTER: Why shouldn't I be worried? We don't know the security risks they pose...

    A well-dressed woman walks in holding a mobile phone and some documents. The policeman salutes.

FIRST MINISTER: Just the person we should be talking to. See, the **SECRETARY OF STATE** is here.

SECRETARY OF STATE: What's the argument about?

FIRST MINISTER: It's about the blue people down in the valley.

DEFENCE MINISTER: (*nodding in agreement*) Yes, it's about those illegal aliens there (*pointing to the valley*).

SECRETARY OF STATE: What about them? are they causing a problem?

FIRST MINISTER: Our colleague is worried sick about their presence.

DEFENCE MINISTER: It's my job to be worried. We don't know whether they're warriors, soldiers or enemies in disguise.

FIRST MINISTER: As far as I'm concerned, two or three poor people squatting down there can't possibly pose a security risk.

DEFENCE MINISTER: What if they are spies? I just have this feeling that ...

FIRST MINISTER: (*interrupts*) Don't give way to feelings, my dear colleague.

DEFENCE MINISTER: I just have this feeling that they are here to harm us one way or the other. People like these don't just turn up! Why now?

SECRETARY OF STATE: In a way I agree with you. People don't just turn up for no reason. But look at it this way, people don't just leave their homes and villages or wherever they were living for pleasure but for necessity. That's why I pleaded at the meeting yesterday that we should take our time before sending them back. Let reason prevail...

DEFENCE MINISTER: I'm really surprised...

SECRETARY OF STATE: My position has not changed.

DEFENCE MINISTER: You say take our time, but time is of the essence. What if they are enemies of Fajra disguised as refugees? I'm in charge of the overall security of Fajra and I say we must act swiftly. (*turns to* **FIRST MINISTER**) Would you trust every stranger that turns up at your doorstep?

FIRST MINISTER: Of course not. But what if on the other hand they were sent, as in the prophecy, to make the dream of Fajra come true?

DEFENCE MINISTER: The dream?

FIRST MINISTER: Yes, the dream of Fajra!

SECRETARY OF STATE: That's an interesting way of looking at it.

FIRST MINISTER: Yes it is indeed. What if they are the vehicle for our task of building and living in the "City in the Sky"? What if they were sent to be *the* helpers on our journey to the Promised Land?

DEFENCE MINISTER: You mean the ones that will carry the burden for us?

FIRST MINISTER: (*nods and smiles*) I'm happy you haven't forgotten the prophecy.

DEFENCE MINISTER: No I haven't. But because I'm responsible for the security and safety of Fajris, I must be guided by what I see on the ground and not get carried away by what was prophesied a long time ago.

FIRST MINISTER: We are all guided by the prophecies of the past... it's in our blood.

DEFENCE MINISTER: Honestly, I see the appearance of these strange people as a bad omen. Something about them is not right. (*Pause*)

FIRST MINISTER: Of course, I respect your point of view.

DEFENCE MINISTER: Then why do I have a feeling you're going to do something stupid?

FIRST MINISTER: What do you mean?

DEFENCE MINISTER: That you are going to take a very stupid decision regarding these people...

FIRST MINISTER: I'm not about to do something stupid. I'm about to do something human. I'm a human being and as far as I can see, although they look really different from us, they are human beings too. (*Long pause*)

DEFENCE MINISTER: No! No!! No!!! You cannot do what I think you're about to do! No, please!

FIRST MINISTER: Yes! Yes!! Yes!!! I'm thinking about allowing them to stay there if they ask to do so. I want to help them because they are refugees. I'm not going to get rid of them....at least not immediately.

DEFENCE MINISTER: (*turns sharply*) Have you lost your mind? (*loudly*) Those creatures there aren't human beings. Look at them. Even from here you can see how strange and different they are.

> *Light shines on the three foreigners wearing blue clothes. They stand in silence behind a sign:* **REFUGEES SEEKING ASYLUM**

DEFENCE MINISTER: (*continues*) Actually, I came here to ask for permission to get rid of them. And since they found it so easy to come into Fajra, I want an order to build a high wall around our city immediately. We definitely don't want any more foreigners entering and settling down in Fajra.

FIRST MINISTER: Calm down. To me, they look desperate and vulnerable, as you'd expect refugees to look.

SECRETARY OF STATE: Refugees or not, they're strangers and, as we say in Fajra, strangers are blind even if they have eyes.

DEFENCE MINISTER: The old saying has no relevance to modern realities.

SECRETARY OF STATE: Who knows what fate has in store for us? We might be refugees in a strange land one day. (*she walks away*) I'll see you later, I have work to do. *Exits stage*

FIRST MINISTER: Listen, my fellow Custodian of Fajra. (*walks closer to* **DEFENCE MINISTER**) Let me remind you that our ancestors were once like them....

DEFENCE MINISTER: (*interrupts*) Our ancestors were not that short.

FIRST MINISTER: I don't mean their height. I mean our ancestors were refugees. Fajra, our blessed town, was founded by the survivors of the great trek who were refugees fleeing all kinds of problems. First they settled in the valley and with time moved up here, with the ultimate hope that one day, Fajris would move up there, (*points to the top part of the stage*) to the city above the clouds, our Promised Land.

DEFENCE MINISTER: I know our history. You cannot use that early history to justify allowing these newcomers to settle down there today. It simply doesn't make sense. Our ancestors were genuine refugees running away from persecution. Their lives were threatened simply because of who they were. By the way, when our ancestors came here nobody lived here; it was virgin territory.

FIRST MINISTER: The truth is you and I don't know exactly what happened when they came here, who they met or didn't meet. We only know what they chose to pass down to us.

DEFENCE MINISTER: I hope you'll have time to think through this properly.

FIRST MINISTER: I have thought through it already...

DEFENCE MINISTER: So what if they refuse to leave? What if they see and taste our wealth and glory and refuse to return to where they came from? What if they settle down and bring in more of their kind and start reproducing and before we know it take over our sacred land? What if in the long run they take over the whole of Fajra? Please think about the consequences. One thing I can be certain of is that this doesn't look like it'll end well for us Fajris. (*Pause*) Please take a step back and ponder.

    DEFENCE MINISTER *walks off stage.*

    FIRST MINISTER *(ruminates)*

DEFENCE MINISTER: *(re-enters stage)* For your information, the Defence Guard has been mobilised.

FIRST MINISTER: *(looking rather surprised)* What happened? Why?

DEFENCE MINISTER: To protect our beloved Fajra.

FIRST MINISTER: That's not necessary.

DEFENCE MINISTER: It is. If you're not going to give the orders, I have the powers to act in case of an emergency. This is an emergency. I want to close the doors before we are overrun by more strange foreigners.

FIRST MINISTER: What if they leave because we didn't pay attention to them? What if they're nomads just passing through? What if nothing appeals to them here and they are seeking greener pastures elsewhere?

DEFENCE MINISTER: *(walks to the edge of the stage. Light shines on valley)* Oh my God! Now there are four of them. *(shows four fingers)* This is becoming an invasion...a serious breach of our security... we must act. This is an emergency. *(He looks down again, light shines on people in*

7

blue clothes). They're multiplying like vermin. First a trickle, soon there'll be a flood. At this rate the valley will soon be too small for them. If we don't stop them *now*, if we don't take action *now*, if we don't get rid of them *now* they will stay there, get comfortable and with time we'll be swamped. This is a threat to our existence...

For God's sake, do something!

FIRST MINISTER: (*calmly*) We don't know why they are there. We don't know what made them leave wherever they were before they came here. It is not an easy decision for me. I'm a human being and have come to the conclusion that we all live and hope for something better in life. We must know why they left before deciding whether to let them stay or go. Who knows what brought them here? Who knows what they've brought with them? Above all, who knows what they can do for us?

DEFENCE MINISTER: I'll say it again - these strangers are good for nothing. If they are useful why are they here? Why are they not being useful somewhere else? Have you seen how short they are?

FIRST MINISTER: Of course I have. Don't forget the prophecy. Was it not said that a time shall come when the Fajris shall construct the eternal city of light and live there? Is it not in our daily prayers to make every Fajri live up there in the city above the clouds? Don't we regularly pray that one day we Fajris shall reach the Promised Land? Have you forgotten the dream of Fajra? Was it not said in the prophecy that the people of colour shall come from where the sun rises and that it is with their help that our dream shall come true?

DEFENCE MINISTER: There's nothing in the prophecy that says some very short, ugly strange people in blue clothes...

FIRST MINISTER: Of course there's nothing exactly like that there. (*now visibly frustrated*) But the prophecy was clear when it states: "A great miracle will be manifested when the lights of the city above the clouds illuminate the whole of Fajra and beyond. And it is on the sweat and strength of the people of colour that the new Fajra shall be built."

DEFENCE MINISTER: That does not justify opening our doors to these people.

FIRST MINISTER: (*interrupts*) Did our ancestors not caution us about refusing people in need? Did they not say that people who are different from us shall come and it is with them, or to put it bluntly, on their backs that we shall reach the Promised Land? Why hasn't the dream come true over the years? Simply because no people of colour came to Fajra. Now that we have them here, in front of us, you want me to send them away?

DEFENCE MINISTER: As far as I understand the prophecy, the people of colour refers to the colour of their skin not the colour of their clothes.

FIRST MINISTER: In a way you are right. The prophecy was not clear on that, we interpret it the way we understand it. It simply says, "the people of colour." Because they wear blue clothes, I understood it to refer to the colour of their clothes.

DEFENCE MINISTER: I'm not convinced at all.

FIRST MINISTER: Another part of the prophecy said something like this. There shall come a time when the cursed people shall appear on your land. These are people who have been cursed to roam aimlessly in the wilderness. They shall have neither roof over their heads and no companions; no one shall help them except where they shall be exploited. They shall be enslaved and made to work for every other people they meet. They are cursed and shall carry the burdens of others...

DEFENCE MINISTER: And so?

FIRST MINISTER: The people down there are the cursed people. (*smiling*) And we are free to exploit them for our benefit.

DEFENCE MINISTER: (*walks closer to the edge of the stage, looks at the valley*) Oh my God. There are now five of them. What are we going to do?

FIRST MINISTER: Nothing but rejoice for the prophecy is correct.

DEFENCE MINISTER: Are you crazy? Rejoice?

FIRST MINISTER: Yes rejoice.

DEFENCE MINISTER: Why do you believe in prophecy?

FIRST MINISTER: Simply because prophecies make the future for us.

Light shines on five people in blue clothes standing near a sign: **REFUGEES SEEKING ASYLUM** *all starring at the plateau. The two men stare at each other.* **DEFENCE MINISTER** *looks at audience with open mouth.*

FIRST MINISTER: (*walks closer to* **DEFENCE MINISTER** *and puts right hand on his shoulder*) My dear friend and colleague, sometimes you have to let things work out the way they were meant to. As a Custodian of Fajra, my first duty is to make our dream come true. (*smiling*)

DEFENCE MINISTER: What if they have another faith?

FIRST MINISTER: So? It means nothing.

DEFENCE MINISTER: It means a lot. Look at it this way. If I have a correct and authentic worldview can I really respect someone who has a different worldview from mine? Can I really tolerate others who disagree with me? We must handle this carefully because we always believed and maintained that two faiths could not co-exist in Fajra.

FIRST MINISTER: Why not?

DEFENCE MINISTER: It has never happened before. To remind you, we always said there would be only one faith in Fajra or in the Promised Land.

FIRST MINISTER: What if they have no faith?

DEFENCE MINISTER: Every human being believes in something. (*Pause, looking straight at the* **FIRST MINISTER**) The supremacy of our faith must not be challenged under any circumstances.

FIRST MINISTER: I can assure you it won't. I promise you that.

DEFENCE MINISTER: If we must, we could accept them on a temporary basis only if their faith is compatible with ours.

FIRST MINISTER: But first we have to know what they believe in.

DEFENCE MINISTER: (*scratches his head*) Are they really from where the sun rises? Remember, the prophecy said the people would come from where the sun rises.

FIRST MINISTER: I don't know. The only way to find out is to ask them. (*gestures to* **POLICEMAN**, *points to valley while talking to him, not audible to audience.* **POLICEMAN** *exits down to valley*)

DEFENCE MINISTER: (*paces around nervously*) I think it's a mistake to even talk to them. We should have asked the policeman to get rid of them instead of bringing them up here. I'm not in any way convinced they'll be any good to us. We should get rid of them immediately and build a high wall. They have probably multiplied by now. We have a crisis and I don't think this is the best way to handle it.

FIRST MINISTER: Where you see a crisis, I see an opportunity. Where you see a problem, I see a solution. (*Pause*) Give me one good reason why you're against them staying in the valley? If you can convince me, perhaps I'll change my mind and send them away.

DEFENCE MINISTER: I have many good reasons. (*to audience*) First of all we must guard the purity of Fajra and Fajris. It is not by accident that this place is called Fajra. Our ancestors derived the word from Fajr, meaning dawn, because they believed, as we still believe, that this place is blessed with the magic of the dawn. If you wake up at dawn you'll have a productive day, a pure and perfect day, because dawn is the purest time of the day. Our blood too is pure and must be protected; it must not be diluted by alien blood. Anything that constitutes a threat to our purity must be avoided, resisted and expelled: like the strangers down there. (*Long pause*) Now you tell me, apart from the desire to fulfil the prophecy, why the sudden change of heart?

FIRST MINISTER: I had a dream last night that made me look at the situation differently. In the dream, I was a victim of similar circumstances. It happened in a very dark forest and I was running away from a wolf. I managed to seek refuge in a house because the door was partly open. I told the people in the house that I was being chased by a wolf and they could see the wolf waiting for me outside. The man who interrogated me said he wouldn't allow me to remain in the house because I was different from them. He looked outside and said the wolf is gone and opened the door and pushed me out of the house. I was very frightened but I had to continue walking in the dark forest. And you know what happened next? I came face to face with a lion. I was so frightened I woke up panting. Luckily for me it was a dream. For those people down there, it could be a reality. I don't want to send them away just yet. I might be sending them to a greater danger than that which they left. People don't just walk around and arrive at a place like this empty handed with only the clothes on their backs. They must be refugees. It's inhuman to send refugees away, into to the unknown. We don't know what they're running away from and we don't know what awaits them. It is just not human to reject another human being without any just cause. It simply goes against the conscience of an honourable man.

DEFENCE MINISTER: May I remind you before you get carried away that this is not a humanitarian issue. Please keep your empathy aside and deal with the crisis in a rational way.

FIRST MINISTER: You have to always bear in mind that who and what we are as human beings is determined purely by the way we welcome and share whatever we have with strangers. We must never forget that! Let's not turn our backs on refugees and our tradition of compassion.

Mobile phone rings back stage. **SECRETARY OF STATE** *walks in. The two ministers wait for her to finish talking.*

FIRST MINISTER: Welcome back.

SECRETARY OF STATE: Are you still talking about them?

FIRST MINISTER: Yes!

SECRETARY OF STATE: Well, we have another urgent meeting to discuss them. (*to audience*). In this day and age I think it's time we got comfortable with people who are different from us. My position is that as long as they don't interfere with our affairs, obey our laws and don't undermine our security and prosperity, that's fine. As a Fajri, I'm confident enough to welcome a stranger. I don't feel threatened and I'm not afraid of difference. (*looking at* **FIRST MINISTER**) I think it's all down to how we consider and classify people. If we consider them refugees they'll be guaranteed protection. So: are they refugees or migrants?

DEFENCE MINISTER: They are migrants who are here to...

SECRETARY OF STATE: (*continues*) The trick is in the language. Are they refugees or migrants? When they are kept down there is it an act of prevention or detention? Are we going to build a wall or a fence? Should we put them in prison or quarantine? Are they assets or liabilities? Are the threats real or imaginary?

FIRST MINISTER: You are absolutely right. Asylum seeker or migrant? Forced migrant or economic migrant?

SECRETARY OF STATE: (*smiling*) The answers are determined by where they come from and why. Humans are always on the move, but we need to know what historical or economic factors forced them to leave their homes. (*Pause*) As long as we build a wall, a fence or whatever to separate us from them, that's fine with me. We must show them we're different and they are different too.

FIRST MINISTER: (*nodding in agreement*) Something that separates us from them. A high wall will do! Let's build one then.

SECRETARY OF STATE: Before we go any further on this, I want to draw your attention to some passages in The Sacred Texts. I noticed from our conversations that you were mainly talking about the prophecy, but what we should be using as our guide is The Sacred Text. (*She picks up a copy from a table next to the flag and shows it to the audience*) This is the most sacred text on Fajra. You see it says, *The definitive guide to the Promised Land and beyond.* And to fulfil our dreams and remain true to Fajra's original aspirations, we should use this book as our guide.

    DEFENCE MINISTER *murmurs something*

SECRETARY OF STATE: What were you saying?

DEFENCE MINISTER: True it's a sacred text, but it's archaic...it's full of contradictions and the language is difficult to understand.

    Phone rings. **SECRETARY OF STATE** *looks at her phone.*

SECRETARY OF STATE: Okay. We're on our way. (*Gestures to the two ministers as she walks toward exit*)

        The three exit stage.

SCENE II

The **POLICEMAN** *marches two men in blue clothes from the valley to the plateau. The* **POLICEMAN** *shouts at them. Four Fajris - three men and one woman enter stage. They walk around the strangers, staring at them. The woman takes a short step closer to them.*

FIRST MAN: Don't go near them. (*holding her back*)

WOMAN: (*she looks at each of them carefully*) Are they human? They're so weird.

SECOND MAN: They look strange but they are human.

WOMAN: They look so different from us that I can't believe they're human beings. (*she walks around one stranger*) See how short they are. In fact, everything about them is smaller.

FIRST MAN: (*pulling the woman back again*) I say don't go near them. (*Pause*) To me they look like aliens.

WOMAN: (*nods head in agreement*) You're right. They're aliens, illegal aliens. (*Pause*) Look at them. (*she looks at each of them carefully*) I'm really terrified of their small eyes. I can tell from their looks that they are here to steal... they're thieves, not refugees.

THIRD MAN: Strange people with sinister eyes.

WOMAN: From now on our streets and houses will not be safe.

THIRD MAN: Even though they're small, they could be dangerous.

WOMAN: I don't like their horrible smell. (*covers her nose*)

SECOND MAN: You're right. Their body odour is very unpleasant.

An old Fajri man walks in slowly with a walking stick. He walks closer to a stranger and shakes his hand.

WOMAN: (*covers her nose*) How can human beings smell like this? Such an obnoxious smell. It's giving me a headache.

FIRST MAN (*covers nose too*) God! They really stink. These are really the smelly ones. I'm suffocating already.

WOMAN: (*looking at a stranger*) What do you want here?

A man holding a multicoloured walking stick steps forward.

STRANGER: We're refugees.

WOMAN: I don't believe you. You're lying. You're thieves.....

THIRD MAN: Parasites....

WOMAN: Parasites with the intent to do something mischievous. I can see it in your eyes.

FIRST MAN: Are you strangers aware that you are committing a serious offence by entering our beloved Fajra and breathing its fresh air without our permission?

WOMAN: Yes, he's right. You're illegally breathing our air, illegally standing on our land and illegally enjoying our glorious sunshine. We'll make sure the Custodians of Fajra deport you all immediately. You're not refugees. You're all lying. I don't want you people here, I can't stand your smell. I don't like your sinister eyes, and your colour scares me. There's nothing I like about you.

SECOND MAN: I also feel threatened by these strange men. The plateau is beginning to feel strange with them on it. Fajra and Fajris can never feel secure with these strange men lurking around. I don't believe they are refugees. I can see in their eyes that they have an ulterior motive. I don't trust them. (*Pause*) Maybe we should not deport them immediately. I suggest we make life difficult for them first so that when they are eventually deported they'll never dream of coming back.

WOMAN: And they will tell others that Fajra is a hostile place for foreigners.

(sings):

What do we want?
Foreigners out!
When do we want it?
Now!

What do we want?
The smelly ones out!
When do we want it?
Now!

OLD MAN: (*waving his walking stick*) It's enough. Stop that! Have you forgotten that our ancestors were once foreigners and refugees?

WOMAN: Who? What? We?

OLD MAN: Yes. Our ancestors were refugees and by all accounts were treated badly by many people during the Great Trek.

WOMAN: (*she walks to a* **FOREIGNER** *with purpose*) Listen you're not going to settle down here.

FOREIGNER: We are refugees. We have no intention of settling down here.

OLD MAN: (*smiling*) Why are you all wearing blue clothes? I'm just curious.

FOREIGNER: In our culture, blue is the colour of the sky and represents harmony.

OLD MAN: When our ancestors came here, they all wore green (*smiles*). See how similar we are?

FOREIGNER: Why green?

OLD MAN: I don't know. Some people said it was a symbol of resistance to oppression they suffered. (*he steps closer smiling*) What time of day is your divine hour? For us it is dawn and that's why we are called Fajris. We are all awake before the first bird sings. We are blessed by the Almighty with an internal switch. What about you?

FOREIGNER: For us it is sunset. We are blessed by the Almighty to be able to sit and enjoy the sunset. Our internal switch helps us relax and sleep throughout the night.

WOMAN: You people are lazy. Listen to him, sit down and watch the sun set. Relax and sleep throughout the night. Lazy people.

OLD MAN: Just ignore them.

FIRST MAN: They're too different from us. I want them out of this place, all of them. I don't hate them, I just don't like them - they annoy me.

OLD MAN: Leave them alone. Let them stay down there. There's room for them just as there was room for our ancestors.

WOMAN: I'm so scared of them I'd have nightmares for the rest of my life if they were allowed to stay here. God help me! What am I going to do? This is the end of Fajra as we know it.

OLD MAN: You'll not have nightmares. You'll soon get used to them, don't worry. And by the way, this is not the end of Fajra but the beginning of something new.

WOMAN: I don't agree with you.

> *(sings)*
>
> *What do we want?*
> *Foreigners out!*
> *When do we want it?*
> *Now!*
>
> *What do we want?*
> *These animals out!*
> *When do we want it?*
> *Now!*

OLD MAN: (*loudly*) Stop singing that song now.

> *Silence*

OLD MAN: (*continues*) It is never right to call others animals. It's not something we want to hear in Fajra. No matter how different other people are, or how angry we are, calling others names and dehumanising them is never right. It's a very dangerous path.

WOMAN: But they don't look human to me. They're strange creatures and we don't want them here. Their stink is polluting the air. I'm already sick from it. Please send them away as soon as possible and build high walls around Fajra. Haven't you noticed that the air is thick with their smell already?

FIRST MAN: Just looking at them makes me depressed and anxious.

OLD MAN: Okay! (*turns to foreigners*) Who are you people?

The foreigner holding a multicoloured walking stick steps forward and replies.

FOREIGNER: We are called Safiyanis. We are descendants of Queen Safiya. We come from a faraway island called Safiyana.

OLD MAN: Why are you holding a walking stick?

FOREIGNER: I'm the leader. Whenever we Safiyanis are more than three in number, we always elect a leader. That's why I hold this stick.

OLD MAN: What brought you here?

FOREIGNER: We're here because we were forced to leave our island after a series of misfortunes. We trace these back many years, to when a new born princess, also called Safiya, disappeared from the palace. No-one knew how a princess could disappear without a trace. She vanished into thin air.

WOMAN: (*interrupts*) Don't tell us stories... lies!

FOREIGNER: Honestly it happened. Our elders said her disappearance was a sign of untold hardships to come. Soon afterwards, strange things started to happen. First we noticed that strange and dangerous animals and reptiles appeared from nowhere and the clouds that decorated our skies started to disappear. Our gracious and abundant rain gradually reduced to droplets and in time stopped falling completely. All the crops failed. We had a long spell of drought. Everything that was green became brown and the once fertile land turned to dust. Many people on the island starved to death.

WOMAN: Liar! Liar!! Liar!!! You're not telling us the truth. (*turns to audience*) Don't believe a word he's saying. He's making up stories.

FOREIGNER: (*continues*) Life became unbearable and people started to fight each other. The island became lawless and chaotic. Then, without any warning, thick clouds gathered and it started to rain.

WOMAN: Why are you here then?

FOREIGNER: The rains fell and refused to stop ...

WOMAN: (*laughing loudly*) I knew he was lying. How can rain refuse to stop falling? Have you ever heard such a lie?

FOREIGNER: The rain fell for days, weeks and months. It was not just the rain. It was the floods that initially drove us out of the island. First the water reached our knees, slowly rose to our waists. When it reached my belly button, I decided it was time to leave. We lost everything because the whole of the island was under water for a long time. When I left Safiyana, I went to a nearby rocky island and waited there for the water to go down.

WOMAN: And the water didn't go...

FOREIGNER: It did.

WOMAN: Why are you here then?

MAN: What happened next?

FOREIGNER: Many terrible things. Climate changed...

WOMAN: (*interrupts loudly*) Climate what?

FOREIGNER: The climate changed. First we noticed that the nights became warmer than usual. Then we noticed that lots of insects, birds and animals started dying without obvious reasons.

WOMAN: What a load of rubbish. The climate changed and it got warmer...rubbish talk.

FOREIGNER: Then we noticed that the sea was rising slowly all around the island.

WOMAN: Another tall story. How can sea levels rise? How can someone lie like this?

FOREIGNER: Honestly it did.

MAN: How did you know?

FOREIGNER: Land along the coastline was submerged, together with houses and trees. When occasionally it subsided, we noticed that there were salt crystals in the mud. They were impossible to get rid of and gave us constant headaches because they made the soil sparkle in the sunlight. It became very difficult to survive on the island; the environment was very hostile. We could not plant anything and the water kept rising and destroying everything including the trees. So I, together with the others here, decided to leave.

WOMAN: Why did you come here? Why not somewhere else?

FOREIGNER: We headed this way by chance. I was looking for any place I could survive as a human being. I had no knowledge of this place. I just kept walking for days and nights until I reached where I'm standing now. (*Pause*) If you don't want me here, fair enough. It's your land. I'll continue my journey.

MAN: Surely the water must have subsided. Can't you just turn round and return?

FOREIGNER: You don't understand. We lost everything and once you set out on a journey like this, it's very difficult to just turn around and go back. But don't get me wrong. We are not seeking home and contentment here. We know we'll never find that. We shall return some day to our island. We strongly believe that it's a cycle.

MAN: When are you going to return? For how long are you going to be refugees?

FOREIGNER: Maybe I should explain why we became refugees. We believe that our ancestor Queen Safiya was the first person to set foot on the island. She loved the island so much that she made sure nothing was wasted or polluted. She strongly protected whatever was in and around the island. Just before she passed away, we were told, she made every Safiyani pledge to look after everything on the island especially the sea around it.

MAN: Why?

FOREIGNER: Some people believed that Safiya emerged from the sea while others said she revered the sea so much because it gave us our livelihood. But as time passed people started polluting and mismanaging our most precious resource. Safiya warned that if we transgressed the sea would be angry and would rise and take over the island as a form of punishment.

WOMAN: Oh my God! How can we stand here and listen to such stories?

FOREIGNER: My generation of Safiyanis did not heed the warnings but continued to pollute and mismanage both land and sea. Then came a very long eclipse of the sun. Our elders said it was a bad omen; the sea was angry and we should prepare for punishment. When the sea rose it seemed it wanted to banish us from the island. So we became refugees. No one knows for how long, but we believe that, just as the eclipse heralded the beginning of our woes, a blue full moon will whisper to us to return.

WOMAN: *(laughing)* You can be sure of one thing, we'll make life so difficult for you that you'll all be eager to escape our hostile environment and return. *(Long silence)* I don't believe anything that came out of your small mouth.

SECOND MAN: That's true. He's a liar.

WOMAN: We don't want you people here. Either you continue your journey or return to your flooded island. There's no place for you here.

OLD MAN: I said it's enough. This is not how to treat a stranger.

FOREIGNER: Of course we shall return. The suffering descendants of Queen Safiya strongly believe that one day we shall all return, in body or in spirit, to our beloved island. The climate will change, the sea will retreat and things will go back to normal. We don't know when but it will retreat. It's a cycle, and when it turns we shall return. We believe the princess is safe and she will call on us — all of us, wherever we're scattered, to return. One way or the other, we'll hear her call. We're not seeking a permanent place to live. We know that wherever we stay will not be our home. To be a guest in someone's house is good, but home is best.

THIRD MAN: *(laughing)* You're a dreamer. These stinking foreigners know how to dream. You dream about living here in Fajra then you dream about returning to your island.

WOMAN: That's a good name for them: dreamers. You left your sinking, chaotic, flooded island dreaming of paradise. You arrived here and when we said we'd make life difficult for you and the you realised this wasn't your promised land, you began dreaming of returning... all you do is dream. The reality is that Fajra is not for dreamers like you. We don't want you here. You don't fit into the landscape and we don't trust you. We don't want to live with your stink for the rest of our lives.

WOMAN (*sings*)

> *What do we want?*
> *Dreamers out!*
> *When do we want it?*
> *Now!*

> *What do we want?*
> *Fortress Fajra!*
> *When do we want it?*
> *Now!*

Enter **FIRST MINISTER** *and* **DEFENCE MINISTER**.
POLICEMAN *whispers to the* **FIRST MINISTER**. *He nods his head and he in turn whispers into the ears of the* **DEFENCE MINISTER**.

WOMAN: Are they going to be deported?

FIRST MINISTER: Not yet. We the Custodians of Fajra have not yet decided what to do with them.

WOMAN: Why not just expel them now?

FIRST MINISTER: I wish it was that easy.

FIRST MAN: Just get rid of them like getting rid of insects.

WOMAN: Swat them off! (*demonstrates*)

FIRST MINISTER: Why?

SECOND MAN: Because I'm suspicious of them.

WOMAN: Because we don't want them here...we're frustrated by their presence. We just don't like them. (*Pause*) Can't we build a wall around our beloved Fajra high enough to keep out these cockroaches?

FIRST MAN: (*shaking his head in agreement*) That's correct. High walls please, Minister. We want these strangers kept out of our blessed land!

FIRST MINISTER: Once a decision has been taken, we shall let you all know. (*Gestures to* **POLICEMAN,** *whispering something into his ears while pointing to the valley*).

The **POLICEMAN** *escorts the foreigners to the valley. The group of Fajris charge forward, shouting at foreigners, trying to hit them.*

OLD MAN: Stop that! (*shouting*) What's wrong with you? (*angrily*) These people are strangers. Have you forgotten the commandment handed down to us by our ancestors? When a stranger visits, welcome him; when he resides among you, do not mistreat him. Treat a stranger as a native. Love him as you love yourself. The arrival of a stranger should not bring out the worst in us. Behave!

Silence

A group of Fajris walk away in silence and exit the stage. The **POLICEMAN** *and the two foreigners exit the stage down to the valley.*

SCENE III

Light shines on five Safiyanis sitting in the valley behind a sign with the words **REFUGEES SEEKING ASYLUM**. *They sit on the ground, side by side, heads down - all in blue clothes - facing the audience. The leader stands up, still holding his walking stick.*

LEADER - As the sun sets, let us be grateful that we have a place to rest our tired bodies. We've come a long way and are lucky to be alive and well. We don't know what tomorrow will bring but I have a feeling they'll allow us to stay, or at least they'll offer us some kind of help. If not they would have sent us away. If they do create a hostile environment and make life difficult for us, we must be patient. We must bear in mind that we are refugees. Let us wear their clothes, eat their food, respect their laws and learn to speak like them. Whatever we go through, let's remember it will be temporary. Things move in a cycle and change is inevitable. The sea will not cover the island forever but will return to its normal level. Princess Safiya will return and once she does, so shall we. (*Stops, looks around.*)

The **POLICEMAN** *can be seen constructing a fence that separates the plateau from the valley.*

LEADER: (*continues*) Look at what they are doing. They're erecting a fence between them and us. (*to* **POLICEMAN**) Why are you building a fence?

POLICEMAN: Shut up.

LEADER: I'm just asking a question.

POLICEMAN: Who do you think you are? Where do you think you are? This is Fajra, not your flooded and chaotic island.

LEADER: Why are you building a fence?

POLICEMAN: We're building a fence to make sure you know your place, to keep you out and to show everyone who we are and who you are.

LEADER: But we know who we are.

POLICEMAN: (*doesn't respond, walks closer*) Now listen, you lot. For the next ten days, you're not allowed to come up to the plateau. You must not cross the fence to our side.

LEADER: Why?

POLICEMAN: We will be celebrating the festival of lights and we don't want any of you to spoil it. The festival is a time to let the light illuminate our lives. We definitely don't want you defiling it. So, I repeat, for the next ten days, don't cross over this fence.

LEADER: What are we going to do?

POLICEMAN: I don't know. I only follow orders. Your fate is in the hands of the First Minister. Left to me I would have sent you away already. (*continues to work on the fence*)

> The **POLICEMAN** *exits the stage when work on the fence is complete, smiling.*

> *A long silence.*

> The **POLICEMAN** *returns with boxes and start throwing clothes over the fence.*

POLICEMAN: You must all change your clothes. Blue clothes are no longer allowed in Fajra. (*throws bars of soap*) And wash yourselves, you smelly foreigners. Maybe your stink will go away with time, but meanwhile we certainly don't want you on the plateau. We don't want your darkness to come between us and our source of light.

LEADER: Do you really have to say all these things?

POLICEMAN: I can say what I want. This is my land. I'm a Fajri. (*He looks at the leader closely and walks closer to him*) Now give me your stick.

LEADER: Why?

POLICEMAN: You're not on your island, you're in Fajra now. You're not a leader here. (*extends his left hand*) We're not going to tolerate your symbols here.

LEADER: Can you please receive it with your right hand?

POLICEMAN: Why?

LEADER: It is a sign of disrespect to give or receive something with the left hand.

POLICEMAN: Where?

LEADER: In Safiyana.

POLICEMAN: Where do you think you are? Let me remind you, you're in Fajra and this is how we do things here. (*shouts, extending his left hand*) Give me the stick!

The leader hands over the stick. **POLICEMAN** *receives with left hand and exits stage*

Lights out.

END OF ACT ONE

ACT TWO
SCENE I

The setting is exactly as in Act One, Scene I. **FIRST MINISTER** *is sitting behind desk, writing.* **SECRETARY OF STATE** *can be seen talking over her mobile phone. When she finishes, she sits next to* **FIRST MINISTER**.

SECRETARY OF STATE: I think my position is clear on this. While I'm convinced by your argument that we need people, they must be the right ones. The question is, are these the right ones?

FIRST MINISTER: Only time will tell. There's no way of knowing ...

SECRETARY OF STATE: I agree that our prosperity could be enhanced if we welcome them. But I suggest we build a wall to make sure we maintain our difference. You understand the need for separation?

FIRST MINISTER: Yes I do and thanks for your understanding.

SECRETARY OF STATE: Good, then I'll be off. (*she stands up and exits stage*)

Moments later voices can be heard back stage.

DEFENCE MINISTER: Can I come in? (*walks onto stage*)

FIRST MINISTER: Of course you can. (*turns in his chair, stands up*)

They shake hands.

DEFENCE MINISTER: I'm sure you've heard the good news.

FIRST MINISTER: Which one? There's so much good news in Fajra these days.

DEFENCE MINISTER: About the mineral resources our prospectors have found in the valley.

FIRST MINISTER: Oh yes. I have.

DEFENCE MINISTER: Great news isn't it? Think what it'll do for the economy.

FIRST MINISTER: Yes it is. What's more, now we have cheap labour to extract the resources. Working in the mines is a job for lowly creatures like the strangers down there. Look at their size compared to ours and you'll see that they're built for it. (*Pause*) As I've told you on more than one occasion, the strangers are God-sent; they're our salvation. They came here for a better life, and we'll use them to better our lives. (*Long pause, whispers*) The truth is that we need them more than they need us.

DEFENCE MINISTER: What a coincidence! The foreigners arrive and minerals are found right there in the valley.

FIRST MINISTER: I don't think things happen by coincidence. They are definitely not here by accident. Fate has designed it that they come here for a purpose - to dig out the riches for us. They are the cursed ones of the prophecy, there is no doubt about it. Why didn't they come years earlier? Why now? Why didn't they take another path that would have led them to another place? Why are they here? The answer is that they're here to be used. (**FIRST MINISTER** *walks closer to the edge of the stage, looks down to the valley*) As you can see, they're happy down there. They're wearing our clothes and eating our food. They are integrating very well.

DEFENCE MINISTER: But still...

FIRST MINISTER: (*interrupts*) Listen, I know what you are thinking. I could get rid of them if I wanted. All I have to do is give an order and they'll be out of sight for good. I can stop them from coming into Fajra, make sure they go away and have a life somewhere else. But we may not get another chance to fulfil our dream. Opportunity only knocks once and we have to welcome it when it happens. It's our manifest destiny to live up there (*points upwards*) in the city in the sky and now conditions are right to fulfil that destiny. (*smiling*) The stars are aligning.

DEFENCE MINISTER *sits down*

FIRST MINISTER: (*sits down too*) Let's think deeply about our dilemma - the dilemma of the Fajris. Look around and you'll see that we don't have people able to extract and process the resources and afterwards build the city. You and I know that the young men and women of Fajra haven't got the hunger and enthusiasm for hard work. The truth is we've become too comfortable and they're not willing to work hard anymore. Even to clean their rooms is too much work. The fact is we need more people, and these strangers are willing to do any work to survive.

DEFENCE MINISTER: Are you sure of that?

FIRST MINISTER: Of course I'm sure. They're desperate. What I'm thinking is this: if we want to make Fajra great and make our dream come true, we don't have a choice - we have to find a way to absorb them and to tolerate their presence. (*Pause, looks straight into the eyes of the* **DEFENCE MINISTER**) We need to make hard decisions about what will truly benefit current and future Fajris.

DEFENCE MINISTER: I get it now. The picture is becoming clearer, especially with the discovery of the new mineral resources down there. But still, I have some reservations. We must make sure they don't mix and mingle with Fajris. You know exactly what I mean. Our purity must be preserved. There must be a limit to how close they can get to us. Our blood must not be diluted.

FIRST MINISTER: Of course. I've thought through that already. What I have in mind is a Fajra First policy where minorities like the refugees down there can reside in Fajra in a manner that doesn't threaten our identity.

DEFENCE MINISTER: I'm happy you did.

FIRST MINISTER: (*thinks for a moment, smiles slightly*) I'll be introducing new laws to that effect soon. Between you and me, these will be called biological laws. The foreigners will have their quarters and their movements will be strictly monitored and controlled. We'll make sure they're physically segregated from Fajris. The foreigners will not be allowed, by law, to live on the plateau for example. They must not be seen to share a common space with Fajris. To make it work, all Fajris will be re-educated to understand the importance of purity and why they must not mix with foreigners. Fajris will be taught that they're superior. This will go a long way in ensuring there is no physical contact between us and them...Of course, foreigners will not have the same rights and opportunities as the average Fajri. They cannot eat together, walk together or play together... (*Long pause*) Listen to this and carefully too. No city is complete without a slum to house its poor. When our ancestors came here, they themselves were poor refugees and lived in the valley. With time they became rich and moved up to the plateau. Now there are no Fajris in the valley because we are all rich and live here. As a matter of fact, every city must have a poor neighbourhood for it to be a complete city. The foreigners will be the new poor and Fajra will be a normal city again.

DEFENCE MINISTER: (*nodding in agreement*) A lot of the things you have been saying make sense. Superior beings must have inferior people to look down upon. Perfect. It makes sense. Indeed, we need to give Fajris something to look down on and it will be the foreigners living down there. But tell me something, what if they don't agree to return to their island?

FIRST MINISTER: The idea is to give them a temporary visa renewable every year. When we don't want them, we simply won't renew it. They'll be disposable and won't have any choice but to leave. We'll put many things in place before they're registered but be sure of one thing, I'm not going to make life easy for them while they are here. They'll always be reminded that they are foreigners, not one of us, and that this is not their promised land of milk and honey.

DEFENCE MINISTER: What if, as their leader said, they do go home? Remember what the policeman reported to us?

FIRST MINISTER: I think the whole story of the princess that vanished and the return of the queen is a myth. There's no queen to return. I definitely don't buy the climate change nonsense he was talking about. He was making it up. Sea levels don't rise, period.

DEFENCE MINISTER: So you don't believe in climate change.

FIRST MINISTER: Of course I don't believe in that nonsense, it is pure fiction to me. Look at it this way, if the sea is rising and taking over their island then that's good for us. They will remain our slaves as long as the sea is over their island! Hahahaha. (*laughing*) They'll remain our slaves until the end of time!

DEFENCE MINISTER: I see. I was a bit worried ...

FIRST MINISTER: (*interrupts*) He's making it up, don't worry. Refugees are full of myths and stories. I'm very certain that once they taste life in Fajra they'll never return. They'll be too busy with the day to day struggle for survival to bother about what's happening at home. And meanwhile, we'll build high walls around Fajra to secure our borders and make sure new foreigners don't come in.

DEFENCE MINISTER: Fortress Fajra!

FIRST MINISTER: That's correct. Fortress Fajra! Once these ones find themselves within the walls of Fajra, having a better life, they'll never want to get out. With time, they'll consider themselves fortunate to be within our walls, serving us.

DEFENCE MINISTER: Is that really enough to keep them here working for us?

FIRST MINISTER: We shall continue to improvise, but one thing we shall use to great effect is money. Money is the most powerful weapon you can use to tempt a man. No man ever says no to money. We shall co-opt them into our economy and ensure that we keep them here through greed. They'll want to live here forever under whatever conditions because we'll make sure they don't have enough. The longer they live here, the more they'll embrace our way of life and forget theirs. With time nothing will connect them to the water-logged island they came from.

DEFENCE MINISTER: So what's next?

FIRST MINISTER: We'll administer an oath of allegiance: the strangers will stand before the flag holding The Sacred Text (*Points to hoisted flag*), and swear that they'll be loyal only to Fajra!

DEFENCE MINISTER: That's very important. Only Fajra.

FIRST MINISTER: No dual loyalty.

DEFENCE MINISTER: Of course not.

FIRST MINISTER: Fajra and only Fajra! Then they can go straight into the mines to start extracting resources. Actually, we're ahead of schedule and they're in the mines already. A charity has been set up to look after their welfare; they've been given cheap food and clothing and a roof over their heads. Soon they'll all be given Fajra names for administrative purposes. They'll each be assigned to a Fajri who will be their guardian.

DEFENCE MINISTER: That's new to me. What do you mean by guardian?

FIRST MINISTER: It's a means of control. The strangers will need the permission of the guardian to do almost anything - from coming up here to the plateau, to work, to visiting a doctor when they're sick. They'll be totally dependent on the guardian to survive. And the guardian can send them away at any time without having to explain why. (*Long pause*) One more thing, as from tomorrow, they will officially be known as guest workers. (*Walks calmly to* **DEFENCE MINISTER** *smiling*) Phase One of the dream of Fajra has started. The city above the clouds will soon rise, and the destiny of Fajra will, at long last be fulfilled. One day, you and I will look down from the city and be proud we were the ones who made it possible. We shall proudly switch on the lights that will illuminate Fajra and make it the eternal city of light!

SCENE II

*The **POLICEMAN** paces near a narrow gate in the fence that separates the plateau from the valley. It is dark. He looks at his wristwatch several times. A **GUEST WORKER** approaches from the plateau. The **POLICEMAN** apprehends him.*

POLICEMAN: Have you forgotten the etiquette you were taught?

GUEST WORKER *is silent, looks at policeman.*

POLICEMAN: You know that as a guest worker you're supposed to greet every Fajri in a particular way.

GUEST WORKER: I've forgotten. Remind me again!

POLICEMAN: You're supposed to stand in front of me with your head bowed (*demonstrates*). Now lower your head.

GUEST WORKER *lowers head*

POLICEMAN: Now look into my eyes. Why are you avoiding eye contact? Are you guilty of something?

GUEST WORKER: No.

POLICEMAN: Then look straight into my eyes.

GUEST WORKER: I can't.

POLICEMAN: Why not?

GUEST WORKER: It's a sign of disrespect in Safiyana.

POLICEMAN: In Fajra, when you avoid eye contact it means you're guilty of something. Your conscience is not clear.

GUEST WORKER: We avoid eye contact out of respect.

POLICEMAN: Why are you late?

GUEST WORKER: I was working overtime in the mine.

POLICEMAN: You know the law states that you're not allowed to be on the plateau after sunset. Look at the time. What time is it?

GUEST WORKER: I was told to work longer hours by my guardian.

POLICEMAN: Who is your guardian?

GUEST WORKER: The First Minister.

POLICEMAN: It's your responsibility to remind him of the law.

GUEST WORKER: He gave me a lot of work to do because he wants to meet a target. He said he was behind schedule in Phase One of the dream project. He said the target must be met even if it means I have to work through the night ... he said if the target isn't met, he won't renew my visa.

POLICEMAN: (*interrupts*) You're lying. You're lazy. If you'd worked harder, you'd have met the target.

GUEST WORKER: Why are you being so difficult?

POLICEMAN: I'm not. It's my job to make sure guest workers are back in their quarters on time.

> **GUEST WORKER** *tries to walk past policeman who stops him.*

POLICEMAN: Time to search you. (**GUEST WORKER** *reluctantly removes shirt and shows empty pockets of trousers*) If I find something that is not supposed to be in your pockets, anything you've stolen from the plateau, you'll be sent to prison where you will work for no pay at all. Do you understand?

> **GUEST WORKER** *nods.*

> **POLICEMAN** *checks pockets.*

GUEST WORKER: (*protests*) I don't like the way you're treating me.

POLICEMAN: What do you mean?

GUEST WORKER: You're treating me as if I'm a thief.

POLICEMAN: But all you guest workers are thieves.

GUEST WORKER: We're not. Please show some respect.

POLICEMAN: You may not like what I'm saying but I really don't care, I can say what I want. If you don't like it, you're free to go back to your flooded island.

GUEST WORKER: I'm a human being like you, please treat me with respect.

POLICEMAN: Shut up. You think you're a human being?

GUEST WORKER *looks at him closely, does not reply but murmurs under his breath.*

POLICEMAN: (*very sternly*) Don't look at me like that and don't talk to me like we're equals. I'm a superior person. I'm a Fajri, so don't insult me.

GUEST WORKER: What makes you think I'm insulting you? After all you don't understand my language.

POLICEMAN: You know it's an offence to speak your language on the plateau. It's not allowed. You must speak the language I understand...off you go to the valley... Know your place and never argue with a superior person.

GUEST WORKER (*clenched fist in the air*) We shall return one day! We shall be free some day!

POLICEMAN: If I hear those sentences again, you'll be going to jail tonight. You know that you're not allowed to say them.

GUEST WORKER *looks at the policeman, laughs scornfully.*

POLICEMAN: You should be grateful you're here, so show gratitude and don't disrespect us.

GUEST WORKER: (*standing in front of the* **POLICEMAN**) We don't have any debt to repay.

POLICEMAN: Were it not for our generosity you'd be starving somewhere in the wilderness.

GUEST WORKER: It's you Fajris who should be grateful we're here...

POLICEMAN: (*interrupts, shouting*) Shut up! You should be grateful you're standing on dry land, breathing fresh air and not stranded on your flooded, contaminated island. You should be grateful you have a roof over your head and a guardian protecting you. (*shouts*) Now sing the gratitude song.

GUEST WORKER: (*grudgingly*) *I'm lucky, I'm grateful. I'm a guest worker.*

POLICEMAN: Again and louder, parasite.

GUEST WORKER *is silent*

POLICEMAN: Again and louder. Remember you're supposed to stand straight, with your shoulders back. Now sing it again. (**POLICEMAN** *repeats himself angrily*) Again and louder, parasite!

GUEST WORKER: (*obeying*) *I'm lucky. I'm grateful. I'm a guest worker.*

POLICEMAN: (*stares at* **GUEST WORKER** *sternly*) You ungrateful lot. You're supposed to be on your knees thanking us for taking you in.

GUEST WORKER: We were human beings in distress and danger, something that can happen to any one. What you did by taking us in was a basic human obligation. It was your duty to open the door for us when we knocked. We didn't ask you to give up anything...

POLICEMAN: (*interrupts*) Shut up or I'll make you sing the song again, you ungrateful maggot.

GUEST WORKER: The earth's main source of energy, without which we cannot survive, is the sun. Yet it has never asked the earth and everything in it to show gratitude. You should learn from that.

POLICEMAN: What are you talking about? The earth is not a parasite like you foreigners. The earth revolves around the sun from a great distance. You foreigners are here on our land, sucking on us like leeches and eating our town like termites.

GUEST WORKER: Remember all things change; in future something could happen to turn you also into refugees. We're not here forever. We await the cycle. When the sea level goes down we shall return home...

POLICEMAN: Rubbish. We're Fajris, which means we're specially blest, not cursed like you are. This is our land. Go down now and learn to stay in your place and shut up. (*walks closer to* **GUEST WORKER** *wagging his finger and threatening*) Either you learn to respect your master or I'll deal with you. (*clenches his fist and shouts*) Know your place. Go down to the valley now.

GUEST WORKER: One day you'll understand our true value, and when that day comes you'll appreciate our presence and regret what you've just said. One day also we shall return home... (*voice fades as he exits to valley*)

POLICEMAN: Nonsense.

SCENE III

The scene is the same as Scene I. Time has elapsed. **FIRST MINISTER**
sitting behind the desk. Three banners can be seen hanging. One reads:
PHASE 2 OF THE DREAM PROJECT. *Another reads:* **DREAM CITY**
UNDER CONSTRUCTION *hanging on scaffolding on the top part of*
the stage. Another banner hangs on the staircase to the top part of the
stage and reads: **INTEGRATION & DIVERSITY MAKE DREAMS**
COME TRUE!

The **DEFENCE MINISTER** *enters holding documents.* **POLICEMAN**
salutes.

FIRST MINISTER: *(stands up, smiling)*

DEFENCE MINISTER: How are you, trusted Custodian of our
beloved Fajra, the man with the most wonderful ideas, destined to lead
us straight to our Promised Land.

FIRST MINISTER: How lovely to see you again, my respected
colleague.

DEFENCE MINISTER: Congratulations for successfully completing
Phase One of the dream project. What an astonishing success over a very
short period of time. Overall, I'm really impressed and happy with what
has been achieved.

FIRST MINISTER: Thank you. The best is actually yet to come.
So many things are coming together to make the dream come true. By
Phase Three all of us Fajris will be living blissfully in the city in the
sky, a special place exclusively reserved for us! Living, as written in the
prophecy, in peace, abundance and leisure.

DEFENCE MINISTER: At last, we'll all be settled in our Promised
Land and make Fajra the eternal city of light.

They both sit down.

DEFENCE MINISTER: Now, before you take me through the draft laws, tell me, how can we afford these gigantic projects? They look expensive to me.

FIRST MINISTER: Everything is affordable if there's the will. We have to be more creative, think differently. This project will pay for itself and we'll make huge profits by the time we're in Phases Three and Four. Fajra will be considerably richer in the near future.

DEFENCE MINISTER: What do you mean?

FIRST MINISTER: I have devised a plan and will explain while taking you through the draft laws. They're interconnected.

DEFENCE MINISTER: I'm listening.

FIRST MINISTER: The first law is to do with the status of the guest workers. We must make changes to their status to enable them move freely in and around Fajra. We need them to go up there to the city to work without obtaining permission all the time. At the moment their movements are restricted and these restrictions are slowing down and affecting our work up there.

DEFENCE MINISTER: But wait a minute. It says here they can move freely and settle down on the plateau...invite not more than two relatives to join them... what's going on?

FIRST MINISTER: Hold your horses. We have to make painful sacrifices to make big dreams come true. No one ever said the path to the Promised Land would be smooth or without sacrifice. We need the guest workers to work to the limit of their capacity, and for that we must create favourable conditions for them to flourish. In the end, it is in our own interest to allow them to enjoy some of the privileges reserved for Fajris, to make them feel at home, to reward them for the work they are doing. If we don't continue to entice them, they might just decide to leave one day. That would be our worst nightmare realised because (*whispers*) we need them more than they need us.

DEFENCE MINISTER: (*looking baffled*) Really?

FIRST MINISTER: That's the truth. Now look at the second part of the document.

DEFENCE MINISTER: My worry is how Fajris will take it. A lot of them will be opposed to such changes.

FIRST MINISTER: Why?

DEFENCE MINISTER: After teaching them that they're superior to the guest workers how are you going to tell them to live side by side with them, and that they're equal before the law?

FIRST MINISTER: One way or the other we have to explain the changes to them. We've got to convince them that the end justifies the means. (*Pause*) Look carefully at the second draft law and you'll see a catch. For the guest workers to enjoy the benefits of the new law, they must all obtain what is called a settlement loan.

DEFENCE MINISTER: What's that?

FIRST MINISTER: As you know the Custodians of Fajra created a bank called Humanitarian Bank of Fajra. Every guest worker must obtain a loan from the bank to buy a house in the valley. It is compulsory. And look, (*shows him a place in the document*) the interest they'll pay will be five times more than what an average Fajri would have paid. This source of income plus the money we make from the mines is how we're going to finance the construction of the city on the hills. Based on our calculations, by the time we move to the city, the interest from the settlement loans will have paid for everything and we'll begin to make a profit.

DEFENCE MINISTER: You mean it'll all be paid for by the guest workers?

FIRST MINISTER: (*smiling*) That's correct.

DEFENCE MINISTER: (*smiling*) That's clever, very clever indeed,

FIRST MINISTER: I told you everything is affordable if there's the will. See, we have the resources. We have cheap and cheerful labour and by this means, we're using it to generate capital.

DEFENCE MINISTER: I'm still unsure of the wisdom of allowing more guest workers into Fajra.

FIRST MINISTER: The reasoning is simple. If we want guest workers to pay for the construction and maintenance of the new city and make money for us on top of that, we need more of them, not fewer. The bank needs more guest workers to borrow more money at very high interest rates to finance the city, that's the way it works. Both cheap labour and cheap capital will have to continue to increase or else the bank will collapse and die. Now we wouldn't want that, would we?

DEFENCE MINISTER: Of course not. The bank must survive at all costs.

FIRST MINISTER: For the bank, it's expand or die!

DEFENCE MINISTER: What if the loans tie them down to Fajra for a long time…Are they temporary loans? My worry is if they get a long-term loan, they'll be here for a long time. Is there an option to get rid of them before they can repay the loans and feel settled?

FIRST MINISTER: I wish it was that easy. We've reached the conclusion that to build the city we need a steady supply of cheap labour and capital over a long period of time. Either we make Fajris provide it by working themselves, or we find a way to make the guest workers do it. One way or the other the city has to be paid for. By forcing them to take this loan and buy homes, they're not only regenerating the valley, they are providing us with the necessary finances to build the city.

DEFENCE MINISTER: So this loan is like an invisible chain…

FIRST MINISTER: (*nods and smiles*) Now you get it. Yes, it's a big invisible chain around their necks. (*laughs*). It's a well set-up trap for the guest workers.

DEFENCE MINISTER: And they will gladly walk into it.

FIRST MINISTER: Of course. They have no alternative. They'll not only walk happily into the trap, they'll be grateful they did.

DEFENCE MINISTER: (*nods and smiles*) Now I get it.

FIRST MINISTER: Other than forcing the loan on them, there's no other effective way of keeping them here in Fajra to serve us and our interests. Debt is a chain and the debtor is always a slave. The guest workers are cursed to be slaves, cursed to carry the burdens of others. The added chain makes no difference to them but means a lot to us. Fate has made us their masters and them our oppressed class. So don't worry on that score.

DEFENCE MINISTER: I see.

FIRST MINISTER: We will change their status on paper but in reality we are making them our slaves. By letting them buy the houses in the valley with borrowed money, we are selling them the illusion that they are stakeholders in Fajra. The truth is the bank will own the houses until the debts are fully paid and meanwhile, they are designed to be repaid over two generations. (*shows two fingers and repeats*) Two generations! The bank can change the interest rates and massage the figures without them knowing. Once they have signed up for the loan, the Humanitarian Bank can do whatever it wants. It's all in the small print which is too small for them to read and understand anyway.

DEFENCE MINISTER: Hmm. What if they do read the small print and discover ....

FIRST MINISTER: (*interrupts laughing loudly*) Those nonentities won't understand anything in the documents, let alone the small print. We'll make sure they never have the education. So don't worry, I can assure you they'll never find out. And if they do it'll be too late...there's no get-out clause. But do you really think those cursed people could fathom such a perfect plan? They're as thick as mud. They are fools and will remain fools forever.

DEFENCE MINISTER: And you said the loan is compulsory?

FIRST MINISTER: (*confidently*) Yes, it is. Every guest worker must get the loan; they can't do anything without it. From now on, their bank account number will be their ID number. Without the loan, they'll have nowhere to live; they won't be able to work or move around in Fajra because they'll have no right to be here. The bank's green passbook will now serve as their passport. It will have all their details in it. The loan makes them stakeholders; without it, it will be illegal to live in Fajra.

DEFENCE MINISTER: What do you mean?

FIRST MINISTER: They have to see themselves in the project, to feel they are part of the Fajra dream and have a stake in the progress of their adopted town. (*Pause*) If you don't give them a stake in something as grand as this, they're likely to feel left out and rebel against it or undermine it. It's human nature. In our case, the best way to make them part of it is to force them to take the loan and make them work to repay it with interest. Once they're in debt, they're enslaved to the city up there. Slaves hardly revolt. Debtors are always loyal to their creditors. Once they sign up to the loan, they'll spend the rest of their lives thinking how to repay it and the harder they work to repay it, the harder we'll make it for them. This is how we'll suck them in!

DEFENCE MINISTER: (*admiringly*) This is amazing. What an innovative way of controlling them! But what if for some reason they can't pay?

FIRST MINISTER: (*smiling*) There's always a price to pay. For those who can't pay, we'll simply lock them up in our debtor's prison for a while before we deport them and repossess their houses. There are others queuing up to borrow from the bank and buy the houses.

DEFENCE MINISTER: Whao! Another brilliant idea.

FIRST MINISTER: The guest workers will own the houses but not the land on which they're built. The Custodians of Fajra will own the land and the guest workers will have to pay rent for it. And don't forget, the beauty of it all is that we can get rid of any of them anytime we want. As I said, it's all in the draft laws!

    DEFENCE MINISTER *scratching his head*

FIRST MINISTER: What's the matter? What is not clear?

DEFENCE MINISTER: I'm trying to figure this out. Let me try and explain it to myself in plain language. So the real-estate finance will be in our hands and enrich us at their expense.

FIRST MINISTER: That's correct.

DEFENCE MINISTER: At the moment Fajris buy homes with subsidized mortgages but guest workers will be excluded from this scheme.

FIRST MINISTER: That's right. Because they're not Fajris.

DEFENCE MINISTER: So what's the excuse for not including them?

FIRST MINISTER: (*thinks for a while*) As you know since they settled in the valley, it has become a dangerous place, not safe for Fajris. So, because they live in a no-go zone, guest workers are not entitled to the loan guarantees ordinary Fajris enjoy. That's one of the small-print clauses.

DEFENCE MINISTER: I see. As always, the devil is in the detail.

FIRST MINISTER: In the detail, indeed!

DEFENCE MINISTER: Let me get this straight. The sale price for the houses and effective interest rate are wildly inflated.

FIRST MINISTER: Yes. They have to be for the model to work.

DEFENCE MINISTER: I see. The model is designed to work for us not for them.

FIRST MINISTER: As I said, they came here for a better life and we shall use them to make our lives better.

DEFENCE MINISTER: And we the Custodians have the power to evict whoever misses even a single payment.

FIRST MINISTER: (*nodding*) That's right, or lock them up in the debtor's prison.

    DEFENCE MINISTER *is silent looking at the audience.*

FIRST MINISTER: Something is bothering you I can tell.

DEFENCE MINISTER: You're right. Something is bothering me but it has nothing to do with your plans to make them stakeholders...

FIRST MINISTER: What is it then?

DEFENCE MINISTER: Some of us have noticed that the inner voice that speaks to every Fajri - the divine wake-up call that we hear before any bird sings at dawn - is fading. Something is interfering with our inner switch so that Fajris are not waking up at dawn any longer...but the fact that we are sleeping later is not a trivial thing. If we are Fajris because we wake up at dawn, what are we if we don't? Dawn denotes purity, good health, prosperity, clarity, vitality and wealth. We are losing our connection to our bodies and to nature and, as we say in Fajra, whoever loses touch with self and nature loses touch with life. Something is responsible for the change and we cannot pretend that it has nothing to do with the guest workers.

FIRST MINISTER: I don't see any connection at all between the inner switch and the guest workers. Speaking for myself, I haven't noticed any change. If anything, I wake up earlier. I'm so excited about this project that I can't wait to jump out of bed before dawn. I think if your personal dream is aligned to the Fajra dream, you'll be wide awake before dawn.

DEFENCE MINISTER: You don't seems to understand what I'm saying...

FIRST MINISTER: (*interrupts*) I assure you that I do understand. But if we're to fulfil the dream of Fajra we have to use the guest workers. We can't do it alone. The simple truth is we don't have enough people to live, work and make Fajra what it is destined to be. Also, we've reached the point where we can't get rid of them without abandoning the project halfway. That's not the way to do things. And anyway, I don't see a connection between them and the inner switch.

DEFENCE MINISTER: Believe me there is. Our way of life is changing in a way that threatens our very survival.

FIRST MINISTER: If there is a link then see it as part of the price we have to pay.

DEFENCE MINISTER: It's a steep price.

FIRST MINISTER: About which I can do nothing.

DEFENCE MINISTER: You can. You can accept that for the sake of a distant dream you're allowing too many strangers in and giving them too many privileges.

FIRST MINISTER: For God's sake, it's no longer a distant dream. Look at the stairs, the scaffolding...We're almost there...We're counting down to the day the lights will be officially switched on to make the city up there the eternal city of light. What's wrong with you?

DEFENCE MINISTER: Believe me, the mood among Fajris is very ... there are lots of angry locals out there and sooner or later we'll have to deal with their anger and resentment.

FIRST MINISTER: Why are they angry?

DEFENCE MINISTER: They don't like the effect of the guest workers on Fajra.

    SECRETARY OF STATE *enters hurriedly.*

SECRETARY OF STATE: Sorry to interrupt you but I have an urgent matter to report. (*shows a file marked Top Secret*)

FIRST MINISTER: What is it?

SECRETARY OF STATE: A geological report on Fajra.

FIRST MINISTER: What's it saying?

SECRETARY OF STATE: A comprehensive geological survey of Fajra has revealed that excessive mining in the valley has created structural defects in the environment, including the foundations of the new city. The experts have identified cracks in and around the new city and have concluded that if mining is not stopped immediately and the whole building project abandoned, the cracks could widen with unpredictable consequences.

FIRST MINISTER: Okay, thanks I'll look at it later.

SECRETARY OF STATE: Please don't delay.

    FIRST MINISTER *waves her away.*

    SECRETARY OF STATE *exits.*

FIRST MINISTER: (*stands looking at the audience*) How on earth can extracting resources from the mines down there affect the foundations of the city up there? I don't see the connection. I suspect a conspiracy on the part of those who are against the dream project. (*sits down, continues*) Back to you. It seems we have a lot of explaining to do then. (*Pause*) Though I can't understand why anyone would object to increasing the prosperity of Fajra. It simply doesn't make sense. Look at what we've achieved so far, just by converting refugees into economic beings whose specific role is to serve our economic interests. Look at them from this perspective and the picture is clear.

DEFENCE MINISTER: Yes, but the ordinary Fajri doesn't see it like that.

FIRST MINISTER: (*angrily*) Why not? Why can't they see it as beneficial to the future of Fajra?

DEFENCE MINISTER: Having taught them to feel superior to the guest workers, how do you expect them to feel when the same people are allowed to live next to them?

FIRST MINISTER: The truth is they work harder than Fajris and consume more than the average Fajri. As a result, they are serving our economy better than the average Fajri. We are making more money from them...

DEFENCE MINISTER: But we still have to do something about the resentment of Fajris.

A long pause.

FIRST MINISTER: I have an idea. We could give part of the money made from foreigners to ordinary Fajris as weekly welfare income.

DEFENCE MINISTER: You mean bribe them?

FIRST MINISTER: Call it recycling the profits from the dream project.

DEFENCE MINISTER: Well it might work for a while...I'll leave you to think about it. See you later.

Voices can be heard back stage, they become louder. **POLICEMAN** *can be seen barring a man from entering the stage.*

POLICEMAN *(offstage):* No you can't see him. He's very busy with the project. You'll have to book an appointment.

FIRST MINISTER *walks to the door. He talks to the man and urges the group of Fajris to follow him. The group of three men and one woman follow the minister across the stage.*

FIRST MINISTER: How can I help you?

WOMAN: We're here to let you know that we're against the guest workers being given favourable status over us Fajris.

MAN: We're against what you call INTEGRATION.

FIRST MINISTER: Why?

MAN: Because we are losing too many things to the guest workers.

FIRST MINISTER: Like what?

MAN: They're taking over the valley and making it their own. They even own houses there. Imagine, a foreigner owning houses in Fajra. Who'd have thought we would one day see something like this? A stinking foreigner owning a house in Fajra.

WOMAN: Not only that, they've made the place a no-go area. The valley is now out of bounds to Fajris. How on earth have we reached a point where these strange foreigners have taken over the valley?

FIRST MINISTER *is silent.*

MAN: They're taking over our jobs and of course we don't like it. Before these stinking foreigners came, I had a good job, earned good money and was proud to be Fajri. Now I'm jobless and no longer know who I am.

WOMAN: We told you the first day they came here we didn't want them here, and we don't want them as our neighbours now.

MAN: First we were told they were refugees who would be down there for a short period of time before sent being away. Then they were no longer refugees but guest workers. Then they became workers and took over our jobs. They've been upgraded to our equals. Now we're asking how this could happen in Fajra?

FIRST MINISTER: They are indeed here on a temporary basis, that's why we call them guest workers. We need them to build the city up there and make the Fajra dream come true. They are working hard to meet the target.

WOMAN: We want you, the Custodians of Fajra, to answer our questions. We're fed up of hearing about the dream. Our identity and our future are more important than your distant dream.

FIRST MINISTER: It's *our* dream.

WOMAN: Yes well, you're living the dream while we ordinary Fajris are being left behind.

MAN: Let's talk about issues that matter to us, not the dream or how hard the guest workers are working.

FIRST MINISTER: But we can't deny the fact that they are working hard...see the progress up there?

WOMAN: Is it true that the construction and maintenance of the new city has been outsourced to the foreigners?

MAN: We heard that they are now solely in charge of everything up there.

FIRST MINISTER: No, that's not true. I'm in charge. We have not outsourced it to them. It is being considered but no final decision has been taken yet.

MAN: Why don't you employ Fajris to do the work?

FIRST MINISTER: The guest workers have proven to be good workers and we want the project to be completed on time and within the budget.

WOMAN: So now we know, it's all down to money. It's about saving money here so some people can make money there. The truth is out.

   FIRST MINISTER *didn't reply.*

WOMAN: Fajri lives matter too. We thought we mattered most, but now it appears their lives matter more.

MAN: We don't want more foreigners in Fajra. We want a total ban on newcomers. Fajra is full.

WOMAN: We're different from these stinking foreigners and they're different from us. Our differences are eternal and fundamental. No room for integration.

MAN: Things can't go on like this. We aren't meant to mix and blend with them.

WOMAN: Things have changed so much that I feel like a stranger in my own land.

MAN: Is it true that guest workers will be receiving more weekly welfare income than us?

FIRST MINISTER: No, it's not true.

WOMAN: How can we have the same rights as guest workers? How can they enjoy the same privileges as us? How can such things happen?

MAN: We are all confused and angry. We want to take back control. We want to be Fajris again and do things the way we have always done them.

WOMAN: We want to be free from foreigners and make Fajra ours again.

FIRST MINISTER: I understand your concerns. But to change things now is to put a stop to the dream of Fajra. We have to continue as things are or risk having to abandon the whole project. We need the guest workers to work hard so as to make our ancestors' dream come true, and to do that we have to allow them to live in the valley. Let me remind you that they're not permanent residents, they're guests. They'll never be Fajris. Once they finish building the city in the sky, their visas will be revoked and they'll be sent back where they came from. (*Pause*) We are just days away from switching on the eternal lights. I assure you that things will change after that!

MAN: We've heard this story over and over again and their status keeps changing.

WOMAN: What's the guarantee that they wouldn't be rewarded handsomely for building the city by giving them even better status than us?

FIRST MINISTER: They're here for our benefit...

WOMAN: (*interrupts*) We cannot see how their presence is beneficial.

FIRST MINISTER: (*clears his throat*) You said they are taking your jobs but who among you is willing to work ten hours a day six days a week in the mines?

> *Silence*

FIRST MINISTER: Who among you is willing to work 12 hours a day, six days a week on the farms?

> *Silence*

FIRST MINISTER: Who among you is willing to work from dawn to dusk on construction sites for less than one third of what you are paid now?

> *Silence*

FIRST MINISTER: Who among you wants to borrow money from a bank - knowing that it'll take two generations at least to repay the loan and that the day you can't the pay interest, the house will be taken away and you'll be kicked out or sent to jail?

> *Silence*

FIRST MINISTER: We have just announced a new weekly welfare income only for Fajris. Where do you think the money came from? Not from the trees but from the interest the guest workers are paying on the loans they were forced to take. Do you understand now? They work and you are paid to do nothing. They're working for you to have a better life. If we got rid of them, would you be willing to give up the weekly welfare income and work hard for less than what you now receive?

Silence

FIRST MINISTER: The guest workers are building your future houses up there — Those houses under construction up there are for you Fajris, and the guest workers are building them. They have been tied to the houses down there for at least two generations, do you understand? They are building a whole city for you and your children, they are working hard to make the dream of Fajra come true. Now do you understand?

WOMAN: We don't understand! Do you understand that we are under siege? Do you understand that foreigners are taking over Fajra? Do you understand that we are frightened for our future and that of our children? Do you understand that we are not comfortable in our own homes? That we're constantly anxious and afraid? Do you understand that we don't want to hear anything about integration? Do you understand that we don't want more foreigners allowed into our town? Enough is enough. Do you understand that our lives matter too?

Mobile phone rings backstage. **SECRETARY OF STATE** *walks in.*

SECRETARY OF STATE: Sorry to interrupt you but this is very urgent. (*showing* **FIRST MINISTER** *her phone*) This is an alert from the geological society. The cracks in the foundations of the dream city have widened and they have ordered an immediate evacuation of the whole of Fajra.

FIRST MINISTER: You know very well I don't believe in these so-called experts. This is a conspiracy to stop the dream of Fajra from being realised. I'm surprised you have joined the conspirators.

SECRETARY OF STATE: I am only a messenger, I didn't write the report.

Sound of cracks can be heard.

SECRETARY OF STATE: Did you hear that?

FIRST MINISTER: I didn't hear anything.

SECRETARY OF STATE: Have you forgotten what the sacred text said? You always talk about the prophecy, but what about the sacred text revealed to our ancestors during the Great Trek?

FIRST MINISTER: No one understands it anyway because it was written in a strange language.

SECRETARY OF STATE (*brings out a book from her bag and opens a page*) Before the city in the sky is constructed and populated by righteous Fajris, the Blessed land of Fajra shall undergo a transformation. No one shall be oppressed, everyone shall be equal and free. There shall be no discrimination and no one shall look down on anyone. (*opens another page*) The utilisation of resources shall be by consent. If those charged with the responsibility of looking after Fajra put their interest above that of the blessed land, they shall be humiliated. If the leaders of Fajra take more than their share, they shall pay the price. The land upon which they stand shall protest. First it shall shake and then it shall give way, and their homes and all the other buildings shall collapse and they shall perish.

FIRST MINISTER: (*interrupts*) That's enough. Go away and leave me alone.

SECRETARY OF STATE: (*opens another page and continues to read*) It is only through the hard work and sweat of righteous Fajris that they shall reach the Promised Land.

FIRST MINISTER: I've heard enough of that nonsense. Just go away and leave me alone.

SECRETARY OF STATE: I am only a messenger. My job is to warn you.

    SECRETARY OF STATE *exits stage.*

FIRST MINISTER: I'm on the right side of history and my task is to make the dream of Fajra come true. In a few days I will switch on the lights that will illuminate the city, no matter what all you doubters say.

    FIRST MINISTER *exits stage.*

Long silence

WOMAN: (*shakes head*) He's not listening to us. We've had enough.

MAN: He's not to be trusted.

WOMAN: He's changed and his language has changed. He's not talking like one of us anymore.

MAN: He mingles with and listens to foreigners more than us.

WOMAN: How can he say those people are here for our benefit?

MAN: Honestly, we'll be better off without them. I don't want them here. Maybe we should chase them away now...

WOMAN: We trusted our Custodians to do the right thing when they first came...

MAN: And they did nothing. Instead they let more of them in and empowered and enriched them. (*Pause*) We can't trust the Custodians anymore.

WOMAN: They're the only ones benefitting from this dream project.

MAN: That's true. They make money from the loans they forced the foreigners to take. They own the mines, houses, farms and construction sites.

WOMAN: We've got to do something. We can't sit and watch Fajra being taken over by these stinking foreigners. We must take back control. (*Pause*)

MAN: It's not the Fajra we knew.

WOMAN: Fajra looks and feels strange every passing day. I don't recognise my Fajra anymore.

MAN: Fajra should be a place with no foreigner in sight.

A long pause

The group march to the fence.

WOMAN (*sings*)

This is our land
You can't plant your seeds here
You can't have roots here
You can't replace us here
You can't inherit Fajra

Go back to your own land
Where you're free to roam
Free us of your horrible smell
Make Fajra clean and ours again...
Fajra for Fajris only!

END OF ACT TWO

ACT THREE
SCENE I

POLICEMAN *enters, looks around and sees a guest worker coming up from the valley. The* **GUEST WORKER** *is wearing a light blue bandana. He has headphones and a t-shirt with* **HOMECOMING** *written on the front. He is eating something. As he walks past,* **POLICEMAN** *stops him.*

POLICEMAN: Show me your green passbook.

GUEST WORKER: (*removes headphone*) Are you talking to me?

POLICEMAN: Well I'm not talking to myself.

GUEST WORKER: What do you want from me?

POLICEMAN: I said, show me your green passbook, the document that allows you to be here.

GUEST WORKER: (*brings out the passbook and shows him*) Are you happy now?

POLICEMAN: (*looks at the passbook closely and gives it back to the* **GUEST WORKER**) Were you not taught that eating on the street is bad manners? In fact it's not just bad manners, it's extremely rude to talk to someone with your mouth full.

GUEST WORKER: Really? But you asked me questions. If I don't answer you'll say I'm being difficult.

POLICEMAN: Yes, you are being deliberately difficult. You are familiar with Fajri values by now.

GUEST WORKER: Of course but I'm hungry and in a rush to go up there to work. I don't have the time you Fajris have to sit and eat at leisure.

POLICEMAN: There is time for everything. You guest workers don't understand time management. (*Pause*) Why are you wearing that bandana?

GUEST WORKER: I need it to absorb my sweat while working.

POLICEMAN: Remove it.

> **GUEST WORKER** *ignores him, takes a few steps.*

POLICEMAN: (*stops him walking away*) Do you understand what I've just said?

GUEST WORKER: Yes I do. Why should I remove it?

POLICEMAN: You know why.

GUEST WORKER: No I don't.

POLICEMAN: You're not allowed to wear any shade of blue in Fajra.

GUEST WORKER: But that's an old law.

POLICEMAN: Old or not, it's still in force. Go back and choose another colour.

> **GUEST WORKER** *ignores him and attempts to walk away.*

> **POLICEMAN** *forcefully removes bandana.*

> **GUEST WORKER:** (*laughs and continues to listen to music, starts singing*)

Back to where the air is free
Back to where the trees dance
Back to where the grasses sing
Back to where the rains whisper
Back to where the thunders talk
Please take me back home

POLICEMAN: Give them to me. (*forcefully seizes the phone and headphone*)

GUEST WORKER: Why? (*protests*)

> *They face each other, eyeball to eyeball.*

POLICEMAN: We don't want to hear such music in Fajra. We don't want to hear anything about going back.

GUEST WORKER: (*annoyed*) If you don't want me to wear anything blue or sing any song about returning to my island, then deport me.

POLICEMAN: You won't be deported, if you're not careful you'll go to jail. Then you'll find yourself working harder than you do now and losing all your privileges after you're released.

GUEST WORKER: But you can't stop me from longing for my island.

POLICEMAN: Have you forgotten where you are? This is Fajra, not your dying island. You should be glad to be here.

GUEST WORKER: I don't care anymore. I love my home for better or for worse.

POLICEMAN: (*loses patience*) That's enough! Where do you consider home?

GUEST WORKER: Where you feel good is home. You Fajris haven't allowed us to feel good here so we can't consider this our home.

POLICEMAN: In that case where does your loyalty lie? Where does your real allegiance lie? Here or there? Let me remind you that you took an oath of allegiance and signed a loyalty contract. You chose to be loyal to Fajra, and only Fajra. For the very last time, it's against the law to talk about going back.

GUEST WORKER: (*paces up and down, visibly angry*) I don't understand Fajris. (*to audience*) When we first came they didn't want us, now we can't even talk about leaving. Have you ever heard of such a thing? Now to leave Fajra, I have to get an exit visa.

POLICEMAN: (*walks closer*) What's wrong with that? What's wrong with you?

GUEST WORKER: I have my own identity, and it's different from yours. I'm not a Fajri, so who am I in this place?

A group of Fajris enter stage

WOMAN (*sings*)

What do we want?
Foreigners out!
When do we want it?
Now!

What do we want?
Our Fajra back!
When do we want it?
Now!

Make Fajra Free Again
Make Fajra Clean Again
Make Fajra Safe Again
Make Fajra Ours Again

They face the audience with banners raised.

FOREIGNERS OUT

YOU WILL NOT REPLACE US

GO BACK TO YOUR DYING ISLAND

The **POLICEMAN** *stands aside smiling. The* **GUEST WORKER** *exits to the valley in haste.*

WOMAN: (*to the audience*) We ordinary Fajris are fed up with the way these foreigners are being allowed to stay and take over our land. They're changing us and our community. We don't like the way our Custodians don't consult us anymore. They listen to the foreigners more. We don't want these stinking foreigners as our neighbours, we don't want them in Fajra at all. We want to take Fajra back to when it belonged to Fajris; when it was beautiful, peaceful, clean and safe. Now Fajra is spoilt.

MAN: It's time to to take back control of our lives and our town. We don't believe the Custodians are acting in our interests. We don't trust them anymore. They have lied to us. Look, some of them have moved to their dream houses up there in the city in the sky. With their heads in the clouds they no longer think and act in the best interests of Fajra. They've abandoned us here to mix and mingle with these dirty stinking foreigners while they're day-dreaming up there.

WOMAN: We're against the new laws: the one that gives foreigners the right to own houses in the valley, the one that allows more foreigners to come and settle in Fajra and the one that stops them from leaving Fajra without permission. We want all foreigners out! Now! Without delay!

MAN: The Custodians sold us a big lie, saying our lives would be better. Their lives have been better, not ours. Our lives matter too!

WOMAN: It's the foreigners whose lives have been made better. Remember when they came here with only the blue clothes on their backs? Remember how poor and miserable they were? Now look at them, walking around with the most recent gadgets and smiling all the time. They might be having a good life but not for much longer, because we're going to create a hostile environment for them.

(sings)

What do we want?
Foreigners out!
When do we want it?
Now!

What do we want?
Our Fajra back!
When do we want it?
Now!

The group exits, leaving banners hanging on the fence.

SCENE II

Just before dawn. Banners still hang on the fence. The valley is dark. Full blue moon is in the night sky. Four guest workers can be seen chatting. They stand facing the audience rather excited.

LEADER: (*looks at the blue moon smiling*) As you must have noticed, we're all very excited. Remember what I said when we first came to Fajra? About how we transgressed and the sea sent us away to be in servitude? We didn't know for how long, but it was clear it was to be temporary. All we knew was that when we'd been forgiven, the message would be conveyed to us by the moon. Look at the glorious blue moon! See how low it's come, how bright it is. It's come close to the earth and whispered into our ears, 'Time to return.'

*A **GUEST WORKER** enters from plateau showing them something on his mobile phone. They all check their mobile phones and rejoice.*

LEADER: (*continues*) We've just received confirmation through our mobile phones from fellow Safiyanis on the island that the sea has fully retreated and rains have fallen and washed away the salt crystals. The vegetation is flourishing again and life is returning to normal. Princess Safiya has returned and urges all her people to return also. Safiyanis from all over have heard her call and now we too shall return immediately. (*other guest workers cheer*)

A long pause

LEADER: (*looking at empty plateau*) We thank you Fajris for having us here. Some of you wanted us out (*points at the banners*) To be a guest is good but home is best. You can have total control of your town and destiny. You can have your jobs back. You can have your houses back. (*he shows his house keys and drops them, other guest workers drop theirs too*). We cannot replace you. We never wanted to replace you. (*points to the banner again*) Fajra will be safe again. Fajra will be clean again. Fajra will be free again. Fajra will be yours again. Yes, Fajra will be for Fajris only, as we are leaving. And finally, you can keep your loans. (*first they show* *the audience then they all drop their green passbooks*) We don't need you anymore. We are free. We told you that climate, like everything else, is part of a cycle. Now it has changed and we're out of here for good.

One by one they pick up their bags. They all line up and wave good bye to audience. Gesturing with his head as if to say 'Let's go', the **LEADER** *exits the valley. One after the other they all wave and exit the valley.*

SCENE III

Noon. The plateau and valley are empty. Someone can be heard singing in the "City in the Sky". Life is good! Life is great! **FIRST MINISTER** *can be seen climbing down the stairs slowly from the city in the sky. He is singing and whistling.*

> *And now I can say*
> *For all to know and hear*
> *As the glorious sun rises*
> *Life is good and great*
> *Life is wonderful*

When he reaches the plateau, he looks around and stops singing.

FIRST MINISTER: Something doesn't feel right. (*He walks around slowly looking curiously around the stage. He looks at his wristwatch*) Hello, is anyone here? (*loudly*) Where's everybody? Is something wrong here in Fajra? Am I dreaming? Is it morning or evening? Why is the plateau empty? Where is everyone? Is the sun rising or setting? I'm confused. Is something wrong with my eyes?

> **DEFENCE MINISTER** *can be seen climbing down slowly with a walking stick.*

FIRST MINISTER: (*Looks at* **DEFENCE MINISTER**) Thank God I'm not the only person here. (*walks closer to the stairs*) Can you manage?

DEFENCE MINISTER: I think I can make it. (*grumbles loudly*) Where are these bloody foreigners when you need them? I can hardly walk and need support and my home care worker didn't report for work today.

FIRST MINISTER: Haven't you noticed that there's no one around? We are the only two people on the plateau.

DEFENCE MINISTER: (*registering shock*) What?

FIRST MINISTER: Yes, we're the only people on the plateau.

DEFENCE MINISTER: (*walks slowly to the middle of stage. Looks around and looks at his watch*) You're right you know. Where's everybody? The day has dawned and Fajra is asleep? What's going on?

FIRST MINISTER: I don't know.

POLICEMAN: (*enters the stage and salutes*) Morning sirs.

FIRST MINISTER: What's happening?

POLICEMAN: Nothing.

DEFENCE MINISTER: Where's everyone?

POLICEMAN: (*shrugs*) I don't know.

DEFENCE MINISTER: What do you mean you don't know?

FIRST MINISTER: Where have you been?

POLICEMAN: I've been sleeping. I've just woken up.

FIRST MINISTER: I see. (*looks at his watch*) Look at the time. Sleeping till long after sunrise?

POLICEMAN *looks at his watch, remains silent, shrugs.*

FIRST MINISTER: What happened to your inner switch?

DEFENCE MINISTER: Don't pick on him. He's not the only one whose inner switch is faulty. I thought I once drew your attention to this.

FIRST MINISTER: Okay, let's not get into an argument here. We've got a crisis on our hands.

DEFENCE MINISTER: (*looking straight at* **FIRST MINISTER**, *scornfully laughs*) Now you know we're in a crisis.

FIRST MINISTER: If the Fajris' inner switch is faulty and they're still sleeping, what about the foreigners? Where are they? (*looks inquiringly at* **POLICEMAN**)

POLICEMAN: (*shrugs*) I don't know. They're probably in the valley, somewhere.

FIRST MINISTER: Go down to the valley and see what's happening.

POLICEMAN *marches to the fence and exits to the valley.*

SECRETARY OF STATE: (*entering stage*) Well done for evacuating the whole of Fajra. I notice there aren't many people left. We've been warned to leave as soon as possible....

FIRST MINISTER: (*interrupts*) What are you talking about? I've not ordered any evacuation.

SECRETARY OF STATE: Didn't you hear the noises in the night? Loud cracking sounds? Didn't you receive my messages alerting you that the ground we're standing on is giving way?

    POLICEMAN *returns with green passbooks and keys.*

POLICEMAN: This is what I found in the valley. (*showing them green passbooks and keys*)

FIRST MINISTER: This is serious! All their green passbooks and house keys?

POLICEMAN: (*nods*) Yes sir.

DEFENCE MINISTER: But where are they?

POLICEMAN: I don't know. There's no one in the valley. It's empty.

DEFENCE MINISTER: Is this real? Or are we dreaming? (*to the audience*) Can someone explain what's going on please?

FIRST MINISTER: If only I knew. (*Pause*) Let me try. Okay, the Fajris are still in bed long after sunrise....

DEFENCE MINISTER: And the foreigners have simply vanished leaving their passbooks and keys...God help us.

    Loud sound of cracking can be heard. The ground shakes.

SECRETARY OF STATE: Oh my God, the ground's shaking again.

    DEFENCE MINISTER *staggers;* **POLICEMAN** *holds him till he's steady.*

FIRST MINISTER: What are we going to do?

DEFENCE MINISTER: You tell me. I don't know.

SECRETARY OF STATE: (*exiting the stage*) I did my job as the messenger. I'm leaving.

    A long awkward pause.

Song can be heard back stage.

What do we want?
Foreigners out!
When do we want it?
Now!

What do we want?
Foreigners out!
When do we want it?
Now!

A group of Fajris – four men, one woman enter the stage still singing

Make Fajra Free Again
Make Fajra Clean Again
Make Fajra Safe Again
Make Fajra Ours Again

They stop and stare at the **MINISTERS** *and* **POLICEMAN.**

FIRST MINISTER: Be careful what you wish for.

WOMAN: What are you talking about?

DEFENCE MINISTER: He's right. Look, we Fajris got our wish but now we have a big problem.

WOMAN: Whatever problem you're talking about is yours, not ours.

DEFENCE MINISTER: Hang on. I'm afraid it's our problem, all of us...

WOMAN: Our problems will be solved once you get rid of the foreigners.

MAN: That's true. Get rid of them and make Fajra ours again and all our problems will be solved.

FIRST MINISTER: We don't have to get rid of them.

WOMAN: What do you mean?

FIRST MINISTER: They have voluntarily left.

WOMAN: What? Where've they gone?

FIRST MINISTER: They've just gone. (*shows them green passbooks and keys*) They left these and they're nowhere to be seen in the valley. Not a single foreign soul in Fajra.

DEFENCE MINISTER: Do you understand what it means?

They are quiet, staring at each other in silence.

MAN: What are we going to do now? Who are we going to be against now?

WOMAN: Let's go and leave the Custodians to deal with the problem.

MAN: I want to see how they resolve this issue. Let's stand aside and watch.

The group walk slowly to a corner of the stage.

The two ministers stand in the middle of the stage staring at each other for a long time

FIRST MINISTER: This is serious.

DEFENCE MINISTER: Serious? Catastrophic, more likely

FIRST MINISTER: This is my worst nightmare. (*sighs heavily*) What are we going to do now?

DEFENCE MINISTER: (*stares at* **FIRST MINISTER**) I don't know.

FIRST MINISTER: (*after a long pause*) Fajra means dawn but with the foreigners gone it feels more like sunset... it feels like we're going through a very long dark night... the sun has set on Fajra... it feels like darkness at dawn.

DEFENCE MINISTER: Please don't say that...

FIRST MINISTER: it's just as I warned you: without the guest workers, who's going to work in the mines? Who's going to dig the minerals we need for our projects, for the economy? Who's going to work on the farms to produce food? Who's going to construct the city in the sky? Who's going to make the Fajra dream come true? How are we going to get to our Promised Land? (*Pause*) Who will keep the lights on to make Fajra the eternal city of light? Who will live in the valley? Who will work in our homes? Who will look after us?

DEFENCE MINISTER: Who's going to look after a sick old man like me?

FIRST MINISTER: Who's going to pay the interests on the loans? This is serious. We survive largely on the profits we make from the guest workers, so how are we going to survive now? Where are we going to get the money to pay Fajris the weekly welfare income?

DEFENCE MINISTER: What are we going to do?

Light dims

FIRST MINISTER: I don't know. (*he looks up and down and around and stares at the audience*) Is it me or what? Are my eyes deceiving me? Look, it's noon but it's still dark. Hang on a minute, I can feel the ground shaking. Oh my God, I think they're right, the ground is shaking. (*can be seen visibly shaking*)

Loud sound of something cracking can be heard. The ground shakes again.

DEFENCE MINISTER: What's that noise?

FIRST MINISTER: (*looking at the city in the sky*) Something cracked up there. It must be the foundations, I can see houses shaking. Oh my God, the dream city is falling down! Oh, Fajra!

DEFENCE MINISTER *dumbstruck, falls down*

Lights out

Loud sound of something crashing

CURTAIN

END OF PLAY

Printed in the United States
by Baker & Taylor Publisher Services